SHARIA LAW FOR THE NON-MUSLIM

CENTER FOR THE STUDY OF POLITICAL ISLAM

BILL WARNER

SHARIA LAW FOR THE NON-MUSLIM

CENTER FOR THE STUDY OF POLITICAL ISLAM

BILL WARNER

ISBN 0-9795794-8-1

ISBN13 978-0-9795794-8-6

ALL RIGHTS RESERVED

V8.31.10

PUBLISHED BY CSPI, LLC

WWW.CSPIPUBLISHING.COM

PRINTED IN THE USA

CONTENTS

MEDITER-
RANEAN
SEA

SYRIA

MAP OF
ARABIA
600 A.D.

MESOPOTAMIA
(IRAQ)

•Muta

•Tabuk

•Fadak
•Khaybar

ARABIA

•Medina

•Badr

RED SEA

•Mecca
•Hudabiya
•Hunain

EGYPT

YEMEN

N

ABYSSINIA
(ETHIOPIA)

INTRODUCTION

CHAPTER 1

SHARIA IN EUROPE TODAY

When you study Islam in Europe today, you are seeing America in 20 years. Why? The actions by Muslims in Europe are based on Sharia law, the same Sharia law that is beginning to be implemented in America today.

- There are times when traffic cannot move in London streets as Muslims commandeer the streets to pray—a political result based on Sharia law.
- Entire areas of Europe are no-go zones for non-Muslims, this includes the police. These are Islamic enclaves where only Muslims live. The Muslim-only policy is based on Sharia.
- In England an Anglican bishop calls for the rule of Islamic law for Muslims. The bishop is obeying Sharia law.
- In the schools only Islamic approved texts can be used; this is based on Sharia law.
- Christians may not speak to Muslims about Christianity nor may Christians hand out literature. This is a political result based on Sharia law enforced by British courts.
- Rape by Muslims is so prevalent in parts of Sweden that Sweden has forbidden the police from collecting any data in the rape investigation that would point to Islam. Rape is part of Islamic doctrine as applied to non-Muslim women.
- In London, mass demonstrations by Muslims call for the end of British law and Sharia law to rule all people, regardless of religion. This political action is based on Sharia.
- In some English hospitals during Ramadan fast (an Islamic religious event), non-Muslims cannot eat where a Muslim can see them. The submission of non-Muslims to Islamic preferences is based on Sharia law.
- At British hospitals, Muslim women are treated only as Sharia law demands.

SHARIA IN AMERICA TODAY

Here are current and historical events in America that are driven by Sharia law:

- On September 11, 2001 jihadists attacked and destroyed the World Trade Center in New York. This atrocity was in compliance to the doctrine of jihad found in the Sharia law. The attack was a political action motivated by a religious mandate for endless jihad.
- Textbooks in America must be approved by Islamic councils. This is in accordance with Sharia law.
- American employers and schools are met with demands for time and space to do Islamic prayer. These demands are based on Sharia law.
- The American banking system is becoming Islamicized with Sharia financing. Our banking system is becoming Sharia compliant in financial law, but is ignorant about the totality of Sharia law.
- Universities are asked to provide sexually segregated swimming pools and other athletic facilities for Muslim women.
- Hospitals are being sued for not providing Sharia compliant treatment.
- No course at the college level uses critical thinking regarding the history and doctrine of Islam. Under Sharia nothing about Islam may be criticized.
- Muslim charities give money to jihadists (Islamic terrorists), as per Sharia law.
- Muslim foot-baths are being installed in airport facilities, paid for by American tax dollars. This is in accordance with Sharia law.
- American prisons are a stronghold of Islamic proselytizing.
- Workplaces are being made Islamic worship sites through special rooms and time off to pray. This is in accordance to Sharia law.
- Islamic refugees bring all of their wives for welfare and medical treatment to America. American authorities will not act—even when presented with evidence. Polygamy is pure Sharia.
- We are fighting wars in Iraq and Afghanistan to implement constitutions whose first article is the supremacy of Sharia law.

WHY DO WE NEED TO KNOW SHARIA?

ISLAMIC SCHOLARS CLAIM: Islamic law is perfect, universal and eternal. The laws of the United States are temporary, limited and will pass away. It is the duty of every Muslim to obey the laws of Allah, the Sharia. US laws are man-made; while Sharia law is sacred and comes from the only legitimate god, Allah.

SHARIA: Sharia is based on the principles found in the Koran and other Islamic religious/political texts. There are no common principles between American law and Sharia.

Under Sharia law:

- There is no freedom of religion
- There is no freedom of speech
- There is no freedom of thought
- There is no freedom of artistic expression
- There is no freedom of the press
- There is no equality of peoples—a non-Muslim, a Kafir, is never equal to a Muslim
- There is no equal protection under Sharia for different classes of people. Justice is dualistic, with one set of laws for Muslim males and different laws for women and non-Muslims.
- There are no equal rights for women
- Women can be beaten
- A non-Muslim cannot bear arms
- There is no democracy, since democracy means that a non-Muslim is equal to a Muslim
- Our Constitution is a man-made document of ignorance, *jahiliyah*, that must submit to Sharia
- Non-Muslims are *dhimmis*, third-class citizens
- All governments must be ruled by Sharia law
- Unlike common law, Sharia is not interpretive, nor can it be changed
- There is no Golden Rule

THE SOLUTION

This book uses a fact-based approach to knowledge based upon analytic or critical thought. When you finish reading, you will know what Sharia law is. More importantly, you will know the basis of Sharia. You will achieve an understanding of Islam that most in the West do not have. Islam will begin to make sense.

THE THREE VIEWS OF ISLAM

There are three points of view relative to Islam. The point of view depends upon how you think about Mohammed. If you believe Mohammed is the prophet of Allah, then you are a believer. If you don't, you are a nonbeliever. The third viewpoint is that of an apologist for Islam. Apologists do not believe that Mohammed was a prophet, but they are tolerant about Islam without any actual knowledge of Islam.

Here is an example of the three points of view.

In Medina, Mohammed sat all day long beside his 12-year-old wife while they watched as the heads of 800 Jews were removed by sword.[1] Their heads were cut off because they had said that Mohammed was not the prophet of Allah. Muslims view these deaths as necessary because denying Mohammed's prophet-hood was, and remains, an offense against Islam. They were beheaded because it is sanctioned by Allah.

Nonbelievers look at this event as proof of the jihadic violence of Islam and as an evil act.

Apologists say that this was an historic event; that all cultures have violence in their past, and no judgment should be passed. They have never actually read any of Islam's foundational texts, but speak authoritatively about Islam.

According to the different points of view, killing the 800 Jews was:

- A tragedy
- A perfect sacred act
- Another historical event. We have done worse.

There is no "right" view of Islam, since the views cannot be reconciled.

This book is written from the nonbeliever point of view. Everything in this book views Islam from the perspective of how Islam affects non-Muslims. This also means that the religion is of little importance. A Muslim cares about the religion of Islam, but all nonbelievers are affected by Islam's political views.

This book discusses Islam as a political system. It does not discuss Muslims or their religion. Muslims are people and vary from one to another. Religion is what one does to go to Paradise and avoid Hell. It is not useful nor necessary to discuss Islam as a religion.

We must talk about Islam in the political realm, because it is a powerful political system.

---

1   *The Life of Muhammad*, A. Guillaume, Oxford University Press, 1982, pg. 464.

WHAT IS SHARIA?

CHAPTER 2

Sharia law is Islamic law. Sharia is the basis for every demand that Muslims make on our society.

- When schools are asked to give up a room for Islamic prayer, that is asking us to implement Sharia law.
- When a Muslim wears a head scarf, that is in obedience to Sharia law.
- When our newspapers would not publish the Danish Mohammed cartoons, our newspapers were submitting to the demands of Sharia law.
- When demands are made for our hospitals to treat Muslim women in special ways, that is Sharia.
- When our textbooks have to be vetted by Muslim organizations before they are used in our schools, that is in accordance with Sharia law.

The attack on the World Trade Center was perpetrated in adherence to the rules of war, jihad, found in Sharia law. Sharia law is the basis for the religious, political and cultural life of all Muslims.

Sharia law is being implemented more and more in America and yet there is no knowledge about what Sharia actually is since public, private or religious schools do not teach it.

THE GOOD NEWS

The easiest way to learn about Islam is through Sharia law. Through learning about Sharia you are introduced to the Koran and Mohammed in a practical manner.

When you know Sharia, Islam makes sense. Most people believe that Islam is complicated or even impossible to understand, but when you understand its principles, Islam is very, very logical. It is based on different views of humanity, logic, knowledge, and ethics. Once you understand the principles and logic, you not only can explain what and why something is happening, but you will be able to predict the next step in the process.

UNDERSTANDING THE REFERENCE NUMBERS

Before you can understand Sharia, you have to learn about three books that are the foundations of Sharia.

Each ruling or law in Sharia is based on a reference in the Koran or the Sunna, the perfect example of Mohammed (found in two texts—Hadith and Sira). Each and every law in Islam must have its origins in the Koran and the Sunna.

We know the Sunna by knowing about the personal details of Mohammed's life. We know how he cleaned his teeth and which shoe he put on first. We know the Sunna because we have the Sira and the Hadith.

You probably think that the Koran is the bible of Islam. Not true. The bible of Islam is the Koran, the Sira and the Hadith; these three texts can be called the Trilogy.

The Koran is a small part, only 14% of the total words, of the doctrine that is Islam. The text devoted to the Sunna (Sira and Hadith) is 86% of the total textual doctrine of Islam. Islam is 14% Allah and 86% Mohammed.

Sharia is nothing more than a condensation and extrapolation of the Koran and the Sunna. Therefore, it is impossible to understand the Sharia without some understanding about the doctrine found in the Koran, Hadith and the Sira. Turn to any page after this chapter and you will find that most of the paragraphs have an index number.

A classic Sharia law text is the *Reliance of the Traveller*, N. Keller, Amana Publications. (Yes, the correct spelling is Traveller with a double l.) It is very authoritative as it is warranted and certified as accurate by five of the greatest Islamic scholars of today. It is a 1,200 page book, written in the fourteenth century, devoted to such subjects as: political control of non-Muslims, prayer, jihad, wills and estates, punishment, court rules, and land use. It covers legalities and theology.

Here is a typical paragraph:

08.0 APOSTASY FROM ISLAM

08.1 When a person who has reached puberty and is sane, voluntarily apostatizes from Islam, he deserves to be killed.

> *[Bukhari 9,83,17] Mohammed: "A Muslim who has admitted that there is no god but Allah and that I am His prophet may not be killed except for three reasons: as punishment for murder, for adultery, or for apostasy."*

The "o8.1" reference is an index number in the Sharia law text, *The Reliance of the Traveller*. The text is divided into divisions—a, b, c, ... This particular law is found in division o; section 8; subsection 1. With the index number, o8.1, you can refer directly to the source, *The Reliance of the Traveller*.

In the example above we not only have the law, apostates (people who leave Islam) should be killed, but we have the supporting doctrine found in a hadith, a sacred text used along with the Koran. A hadith is what Mohammed did or said.

This particular hadith is from *Sahih al-Bukhari*, one of the six canonical hadith collections of Sunni Islam. These prophetic traditions, or hadith, were collected by the Muslim scholar Muhammad ibn Ismail al-Bukhari about 200 years after Mohammed died and compiled during his lifetime. It is the most authoritative of all the collections. Sahih means authentic or correct. Notice the index number—9,83,17. This reference number is like a chapter and verse index so that you can go and read the original. All of the hadith, including Bukhari, can be found on many university Internet sites.

Here is a Sharia law supported by the Koran:

09.0 JIHAD

Jihad means war against Kafirs to establish Islam.

Koran 2:216 *You are commanded to fight although you dislike it. You may hate something that is good for you, and love something that is bad for you. Allah knows and you do not.*

Above, we have the Sharia text defining what jihad is and then the foundational reference for the authority is provided. Again, you can verify the accuracy of the Koran verses and the original reference, 09.0, in the *Reliance of the Traveller*.

There is one last type of reference to a supporting document.

DEALING WITH A REBELLIOUS WIFE

m10.12 When a husband notices signs of rebelliousness...

Ishaq969 ... *Men were to lay injunctions on women lightly for they were prisoners of men and had no control over their persons.*

Above we have the usual Sharia reference number, m10.12, which relates to the *Reliance of the Traveller*—the original reference. The Ishaq index number, 969, is a margin note reference that allows you to look in the Sira (Mohammed's biography—*The Life of Muhammad*, A. Guillaume) and verify the reference for yourself.

BELIEVABLE AND AUTHORITATIVE

This is fact-based knowledge based upon critical thought and analysis. Everything you see here can be independently verified.

This is a very different approach from asking a Muslim or an "expert" about Islam or Sharia. If a Muslim or any expert says something about Islam that disagrees with the Koran or Sunna, then the expert is wrong. If the expert says something that agrees with Koran or Sunna, then the expert is right, although redundant.

Once you know Koran and Sunna, further advice is not required.

POLITICAL ISLAM

The largest part of the Trilogy is not about how to be a good Muslim. Instead most of the text is devoted to the unbeliever. The Koran devotes 64% of its total words to the unbeliever and the Trilogy, as a whole, devotes 60% of its text to the unbelievers.

Islam is NOT just a religion. It is a complete civilization with a detailed political system, religion and a legal code—the Sharia. Mohammed preached the religion of Islam for 13 years in Mecca and got 150 Arabs to convert to Islam. He went to Medina and became a politician and a warlord. After 2 years in Medina, every Jew was murdered, enslaved, or exiled. He was involved in an event of violence on the average of every 6 weeks for the last 9 years of his life[1]. Mohammed died without a single enemy left standing.

This was not a religious process, but a political process. Jihad is political action with a religious motivation. Political Islam is the doctrine that deals with the non-Muslim.

Mohammed did not succeed with his program of religion, but his political process of jihad triumphed. Sharia law is the political implementation of the Islamic civilization.

The political nature of Islam is what creates the major difference between Sharia and Jewish religious law, *halakha*. Jewish law has nothing to say about non-Jews and explicitly says that the law of the land trumps halakha.

---

1   *The Life of Mohammed*, A. Guillaume, Oxford University press, 1955, page 660.

Sharia has a lot to say about Kafirs and how they are to be tre gated and ruled. Sharia claims political supremacy over the Consu.

There is nothing good for non-Muslims in the Sharia. This is why every unbeliever has a reason to know Sharia law, especially those in politics, policy, regulation and legal matters. Sharia law is about the unbeliever as well as the Muslim. Islam's attitudes and actions about unbelievers are political, not religious.

Even though Sharia violates every principle of our Constitution, it is being implemented today, because Americans are unaware about Sharia or its meaning.

SHARIA AND INTERPRETATION

When faced with unpleasant verses from the Koran, it is commonly said that the true meaning depends upon how one interprets the text. For over a thousand years, the Sharia has been the official and normative interpretation for all of Islam. Sharia is the Koran and Sunna interpreted by Islam's finest scholars. There is no need to look further for interpretation; that work has been done for a thousand years. New matters in Islam must be evaluated and judged according to Sharia, the final and universal moral code for all humanity until the end of time.

The Sharia is based on the perfect, unchanging Koran and Sunna. The vast majority of Islamic scholars argue that the Sharia is Allah's will in the past and the present. It should be implemented by all peoples as the only sacred law in its present form.

Any change or reform of the Sharia must be based the Koran and the Sunna of Mohammed, just like the classical text.

TECHNICAL DETAILS

If you read something in this book and want to know more, most paragraphs have an index number. You can look it up.

Koran 1:2 is a reference to the Koran, chapter 1, verse 2.

Ishaq 123 is a reference to Ishaq's Sira, margin note 123.

[Bukhari 1,3,4] is a reference to *Sahih Bukhari*, volume 1, book 3, number 4.

[Muslim 012, 1234] is a reference to *Sahih Muslim*, book 12, number 1234.

WOMEN

CHAPTER 3

ISLAMIC SCHOLARS CLAIM:

- Sharia laws concerning women are the rule of law in Islamic families.
- Islam was the first civilization to provide and guarantee women's rights.
- Mohammed gave the world the perfect example of how women are protected in Islam.
- Muslim women are treasured and as treasures must be protected from the evils of the kafir world.
- The rights of Muslim women come from Allah.

THE SHARIA: Sharia law has different laws for different groups of people. Women are one of its special classes.

WIFE BEATING

Islam's grand vision about women is given in one verse of the Koran:

> *Koran 4:34 Allah has made men superior to women because men spend their wealth to support them. Therefore, virtuous women are obedient, and they are to guard their unseen parts as Allah has guarded them. As for women whom you fear will rebel, admonish them first, and then send them to a separate bed, and then beat them. But if they are obedient after that, then do nothing further; surely Allah is exalted and great!*

THE SHARIA: DEALING WITH A REBELLIOUS WIFE

m10.12 When a husband notices signs of rebelliousness in his wife whether in words as when she answers him coldly when she used to do so politely, or he asks her to come to bed and she refuses, contrary to her usual habit; or whether in acts, as when he finds her averse to him when she was previously kind and cheerful, he warns her in words without keeping from her or hitting her, for it may be that she has an excuse.

The warning could be to tell her, "Fear Allah concerning the rights you owe to me," or it could be to explain that rebelliousness nullifies his obligation to support her and give her a turn amongst other wives, or it could be to inform her, "Your obeying me is religiously obligatory".

If she commits rebelliousness, he keeps from sleeping (having sex) with her and refuses to speak to her, and may hit her, but not in a way that injures her, meaning he may not bruise her, break bones, wound her, or cause blood to flow. It is unlawful to strike another's face. He may hit her whether she is rebellious only once or whether more than once, though a weaker opinion holds that he may not hit her unless there is repeated rebelliousness.

Ishaq969 He [Mohammed] also told them men had rights over their wives and women had rights over their husbands. The wives were never to commit adultery or act in a sexual manner toward others. If they did, they were to be put in separate rooms and beaten lightly. If they refrained from what was forbidden, they had the right to food and clothing. Men were to lay injunctions on women lightly for they were prisoners of men and had no control over their persons.

[Abu Dawud 11, 2142] Mohammed said: A man will not be asked as to why he beat his wife.

[Bukhari 7,62,132] The Prophet said, "None of you should flog his wife as he flogs a slave and then have sexual intercourse with her in the last part of the day." Most of those in Hell will be women.

THE DOCTRINE OF WOMEN

There are many ways in which the woman does not have full stature in Sharia law:

022.1 The necessary qualifications for being an Islamic judge are:
(a) to be a male freeman [...]

04.9 The indemnity for the death or injury of a woman is one-half the indemnity paid for a man.

[Bukhari 3,48,826] Mohammed asked, "Is not the value of a woman's eye-witness testimony half that of a man's?" A woman said, "Yes." He said, "That is because a woman's mind is deficient."

L10.3 They divide the universal share so that the male receives the portion of two females.

Koran 4:11 *It is in this manner that Allah commands you concerning your children: A male should receive a share equal to that of two females, [...]*

This hadith equates camels, slaves and women.

> *[Abu Dawud 11, 2155] Mohammed said: If one of you marries a woman or buys a slave, he should say: "O Allah, I ask You for the good in her, and in the disposition You have given her; I take refuge in You from the evil in her, and in the disposition You have given her." When he buys a camel, he should take hold of the top of its hump and say the same kind of thing.*

Women are inferior to men in intelligence and religion.

> *[Bukhari 1,6,301] While on his way to pray, Mohammed passed a group of women and he said, "Ladies, give to charities and donate money to the unfortunate, because I have witnessed that most of the people in Hell are women.*
>
> *They asked, "Why is that?"*
>
> *He answered, "You swear too much, and you show no gratitude to your husbands. I have never come across anyone more lacking in intelligence, or ignorant of their religion than women. A careful and intelligent man could be misled by many of you."*
>
> *They responded, "What exactly are we lacking in intelligence or faith?"*
>
> *Mohammed said, "Is it not true that the testimony of one man is the equal to the testimony of two women?"*
>
> *After they affirmed that this was true, Mohammed said, "That illustrates that women are lacking in intelligence. Is it not also true that women may not pray nor fast during their menstrual cycle?" They said that this was also true.*
>
> *Mohammed then said, "That illustrates that women are lacking in their religion."*

A woman's testimony is worth half that of a man.

> 2:282 *Believers! When you contract a loan for a certain period, write it down, or to be fair, let a scribe write it down. The scribe should not refuse to write as Allah has taught him; therefore, let the scribe record what the debtor dictates being mindful of his duty to Allah and not reducing the amount he owes. If the debtor is ignorant and unable to dictate, let his guardian do so with fairness. Call two men in to witness this, but if two men cannot be found, then call one man and two women whom you see fit to be witnesses. Therefore, if either woman makes an error, the other can correct her [...]*

FEMALE GENITAL MUTILATION, FEMALE CIRCUMCISION

It is unfortunate that the term circumcision is applied to both the removal of the foreskin of the male and the removal of the clitoris of the woman. There is no comparison.

> *[Bukhari 7,72,,779] Mohammed said, "Five practices are characteristics of the ancient prophets: circumcision, shaving the pubic hair, cutting the moustaches short, clipping the nails, and depilating the hair of the armpits."*

This hadith refers to the circumcision of female genitalia. It assumes that both the man and the woman are circumcised.

> *[Muslim 003,0684] [...] Abu Musa then said, "When is a bath obligatory?" Aisha responded, "You have asked the right person. Mohammed has said that a bath is obligatory when a man is encompassed by a woman and their circumcised genitalia touch."*

Circumcision is part of the Sharia law. Here is the deceptive translation:

e4.3 Circumcision is obligatory for both men and women. For men it consists of removing the prepuce from the penis, and for women, removing the prepuce of the clitoris (not the clitoris itself, as some mistakenly assert).

However what the Arabic actually says is:

e4.3 Circumcision is obligatory (for every male and female) by cutting off the piece of skin on the glans of the penis of the male, but circumcision of the female is by cutting out the clitoris (this is called Hufaad)."

This deceptive translation obscures the Sharia law. This deception is called *taqiyya*, a form of sacred deception.

At the battle of Badr, we have a reference to the custom of removing the clitoris.

1564 Hamza said, '*Come here, you son of a female circumciser.*' Now his mother was Umm Anmar, *a female circumciser (one who circumcised girls) in Mecca.* Then Hamza smote him and killed him.

O12.0 THE PENALTY FOR FORNICATION

o12.6 If the penalty is stoning, they are to be stoned, no matter the weather, or if they are ill. A pregnant woman is not stoned until she gives birth and the child does not need to nurse.

> *[Muslim 017, 4206] ... There came to Mohammed a woman who said: Allah's Messenger, I have committed adultery, [...] When she was delivered she came with the child (wrapped) in a rag and said: Here is the child whom I have given birth to. He said: Go away and suckle him until you wean him. When she had weaned him, she came to him with the child who was holding a piece of bread in his hand. She said: Allah's Apostle, here is he as I have weaned him and he eats food. He entrusted the child to one of the Muslims and then pronounced punishment. And she was put in a ditch up to her chest and he commanded people and they stoned her. ...*

HONOR KILLING

Honor killing is not directly included in Sharia doctrine. Sharia dictates that a woman is inferior to the male and allows beatings to enforce the rule of the male, but it does not accord honor killing a legal status. However, there is no penalty for killing an adulterer:

o5.4 There is no expiation for killing someone who has left Islam, a highwayman or a convicted married adulterer...

e12.8 ... unworthy (those who may be killed) includes ... convicted married adulterers...

This seems to include equal penalties for both men and women, however, a man has many legal ways to have sex, while the woman is strictly limited to her husband alone. Hence, the woman is much more likely to be killed.

The man rules the woman, and his status in the community depends upon how his women conduct themselves. *Ghira* is sacred jealousy, even Allah has ghira. Ghira is also self-respect and is the basis of honor killings. Notice that in this hadith Saed's threat to kill a man with his wife is not condemned, but supported. Violence in defense of a Muslim's ghira is pure Islam.

> *[Bukhari 8,82,829; Bukhari 9,93,512] Saed bin Ubada said, "If I saw a man with my wife, I would strike him with the blade of my sword." This news reached Mohammed, who then said, "You people are astonished at Saed's ghira (self-respect). By Allah, I have more ghira than he, and Allah has more ghira than I, and because of Allah's ghira, He has made unlawful shameful deeds and sins done in open and in secret. [...]*

Most honor killings come from Islamic societies.

FAMILY LAW

CHAPTER 4

ISLAMIC SCHOLARS CLAIM: The perfect Islamic family law is sacred law since it is based upon the words of Allah in the glorious Koran and the Sunna of Mohammed. All other laws are man-made and must submit to the will of Allah; therefore, only Sharia law is suitable for Muslims. For Muslims to be ruled by Kafir laws is an abomination.

THE SHARIA:

m3.13 Guardians are of two types, those who may compel their female charges to marry someone, and those who may not.

m6.10 It is unlawful for a free man to marry more than four women.

m8.2 A guardian may not marry his prepubescent daughter to someone for less than the amount typically received as marriage payment by similar brides.

ADULTERY

> *[Bukhari 3,38,508] Mohammed said, "Unais, confront this man's wife and if she admits committing adultery have her stoned to death."*

> *[Bukhari 8,82,803] Ali had a woman stoned to death on a Friday and said, "I have punished her as Mohammed would have."*

m10.4 The husband may forbid his wife to leave the home. But if one of her relatives dies, it is preferable to let her leave to visit them.

M5.0 CONJUGAL RIGHTS, THE WIFE'S MARITAL OBLIGATIONS

m5.1 It is obligatory for a woman to let her husband have sex with her immediately when:

> (a) he asks her
> (b) at home
> (c) and she can physically endure it

[Abu Dawud 11, 2138; 2139] Muawiyah said: Apostle of Allah, how should we approach our wives and how should we leave them? He replied: Approach your tilth (tilth is a plowed field, a term for the vagina) when or how you will, ...

The most important thing that a woman brings to the marriage is her vagina.

[Bukhari 7,62,81] Mohammed said, "The marriage vow most rightly expected to be obeyed is the husband's right to enjoy the wife's vagina."

Allah curses the woman who resists sex.

[Bukhari 7,62,121] Mohammed: "If a woman refuses her husband's request for sex, the angels will curse her through the night."

From the Sira, we have some more about a husband's rights:

Ishaq 957 Mohammed sent Muadh to Yemen to proselytize. While he was there he was asked what rights a husband has over the wife. He replied to the woman who asked, "If you went home and found your husband's nose running with pus and blood and you sucked it until it was cleaned, you still would not have fulfilled your husband's rights."

CHILD BRIDES

Mohammed, age 51, proposed marriage to Aisha when she was six years old. Marriage to a child is Sunna.

[Bukhari 7,62,18] When Mohammed asked Abu Bakr for Aisha's hand in marriage, Abu replied, "But I am your brother." Mohammed said, "You are only my brother in Allah's religion and His Book, so it is lawful for me to marry her."

THE KAFIR

Until now we have looked at the big picture of Sharia and then the position of women in Sharia. We now come to a new subject—the unbeliever or non-Muslim. The word "non-Muslim" is used in the translation of Sharia law, but the actual Arabic word used is "Kafir". But the word Kafir means far more than non-Muslim. The original meaning of the word was "concealer", one who conceals the truth of Islam.

The Koran says that the Kafir may be deceived, plotted against, hated, enslaved, mocked, tortured and worse. The word is usually translated as "unbeliever" but this translation is wrong. The word "unbeliever" is logically and emotionally neutral, whereas, Kafir is the most abusive, prejudiced and hateful word in any language.

There are many religious names for Kafirs: polytheists, idolaters, People of the Book (Christians and Jews), Buddhists, atheists, agnostics, and pagans. Kafir covers them all, because no matter what the religious name is, they can all be treated the same. What Mohammed said and did to polytheists can be done to any other category of Kafir.

Islam devotes a great amount of energy to the Kafir. The majority (64%) of the Koran is devoted to the Kafir, and nearly all of the Sira (81%) deals with Mohammed's struggle with them. The Hadith (Traditions) devotes 32% of the text to Kafirs[1]. Overall, the Trilogy devotes 60% of its content to the Kafir.

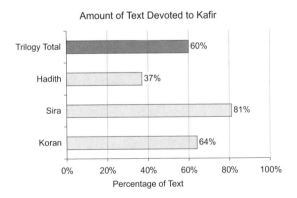

Amount of Text Devoted to Kafir

---

1 http://cspipublishing.com/statistical/TrilogyStats/AmtTxtDevotedKafir.html

The Sharia does not devote nearly that much to the Kafir since Sharia law is primarily for Muslims. Besides, the Kafir has few rights, so there is little to expound on.

Religious Islam is what Muslims do to go to Paradise and avoid Hell. What Mohammed did to Kafirs was not religious, but political. Political Islam is what is of concern to Kafirs, not the religion. Who cares how a Muslim worships, but every one of us is concerned as to what they do to us and say about us. Political Islam should be of concern to every Kafir.

Here are two Sharia references about Kafirs:

w59.2 [...] And this clarifies the Koranic verses and hadiths about hatred for the sake of Allah and love for the sake of Allah, *Al Walaa wa al Baraa*, being unyielding towards the Kafirs, hard against them, and detesting them, while accepting the destiny of Allah Most High insofar as it is the decree of Allah Mighty and Majestic.

Hatred for the sake of Allah and love for the sake of Allah is called *Al Walaa wa al Baraa*, a fundamental principle of Islamic ethics and Sharia. A Muslim is to hate what Allah hates and love what Allah loves. Allah hates the Kafir, therefore, a Muslim is to act accordingly.

> 40:35 *They [Kafirs] who dispute the signs [Koran verses] of Allah without authority having reached them are greatly hated by Allah and the believers [Muslims]. So Allah seals up every arrogant, disdainful heart.*

h8.24 It is not permissible to give *zakat* [charity] to a Kafir, or to someone whom one is obliged to support such as a wife or family member.

Here are a few of the Koran references:

A Kafir can be mocked—
> 83:34 *On that day the faithful will mock the Kafirs, while they sit on bridal couches and watch them. Should not the Kafirs be paid back for what they did?*

A Kafir can be beheaded—
> 47:4 *When you encounter the Kafirs on the battlefield, cut off their heads until you have thoroughly defeated them and then take the prisoners and tie them up firmly.*

A Kafir can be plotted against—
> 86:15 *They plot and scheme against you [Mohammed], and I plot and scheme against them. Therefore, deal calmly with the Kafirs and leave them alone for a while.*

A Kafir can be terrorized—

8:12 *Then your Lord spoke to His angels and said, "I will be with you. Give strength to the believers. I will send terror into the Kafirs' hearts, cut off their heads and even the tips of their fingers!"*

A Muslim is not the friend of a Kafir—

3:28 *Believers should not take Kafirs as friends in preference to other believers. Those who do this will have none of Allah's protection and will only have themselves as guards. Allah warns you to fear Him for all will return to Him.*

A Kafir is evil—

23:97 *And say: Oh my Lord! I seek refuge with You from the suggestions of the evil ones [Kafirs]. And I seek refuge with you, my Lord, from their presence.*

A Kafir is disgraced—

37:18 *Tell them, "Yes! And you [Kafirs] will be disgraced."*

A Kafir is cursed—

33:60 *They [Kafirs] will be cursed, and wherever they are found, they will be seized and murdered. It was Allah's same practice with those who came before them, and you will find no change in Allah's ways.*

KAFIRS AND PEOPLE OF THE BOOK

Muslims tell Christians and Jews that they are special. They are "People of the Book" and are brothers in the Abrahamic faith. But in Islam you are a Christian, if and only if, you believe that Christ was a man who was a prophet of Allah; there is no Trinity; Jesus was not crucified nor resurrected and that He will return to establish Sharia law. To be a true Jew you must believe that Mohammed is the last in the line of Jewish prophets.

This verse is positive:

5:77 *Say: Oh, People of the Book, do not step out of the bounds of truth in your religion, and do not follow the desires of those who have gone wrong and led many astray. They have themselves gone astray from the even way.*

Islamic doctrine is dualistic, so there is an opposite view as well. Here is the last verse written about the People of the Book (A later verse abrogates or replaces an earlier verse. See page 26.). This is the final word. It calls for Muslims to make war on the People of the Book who do not believe in the religion of truth, Islam.

9:29 *Make war on those who have received the Scriptures [Jews and Christians] but do not believe in Allah or in the Last Day. They do not forbid what Allah and His Messenger have forbidden. The Christians and Jews do not follow the religion of truth until they submit and pay the poll tax [jizya] and they are humiliated.*

The sentence "They do not forbid..." means that they do not accept Sharia law; "until they submit" means to submit to Sharia law. Christians and Jews who do not accept Mohammed as the final prophet are Kafirs.

Muslims pray five times a day and the opening prayer always includes:

Koran 1: 7 *Not the path of those who anger You [the Jews] nor the path of those who go astray [the Christians].*

The Trilogy spends a lot of time on the Jews. In Mecca the mention is generally favorable. However, in Medina Jews were the enemy of Islam because they denied Mohammed as the final prophet. Here is the data on the Trilogy texts and the Jews[2]. Notice that the Trilogy has more Jew hatred than *Mein Kampf*.

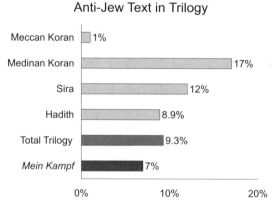

Anti-Jew Text in Trilogy

LANGUAGE

Since the original Arabic word for unbelievers was Kafir and that is the actual word used in the Koran and Sharia law, that is the word used here for accuracy and precision.

It is very simple: if you don't believe Mohammed and his Koran, you are a Kafir.

---

2   http://cspipublishing.com/statistical/TrilogyStats/Amt_anti-Jew_Text.html

JIHAD

CHAPTER 6

Jihad is part of Sharia law.

FROM THE SHARIA:

09.0 JIHAD

Jihad means war against Kafirs to establish Islam's Sharia law.

> Koran 2:216 *You are commanded to fight although you dislike it. You may hate something that is good for you, and love something that is bad for you. Allah knows and you do not.*

> Koran 4:89 *They would have you become Kafirs like them so you will all be the same. Therefore, do not take any of them as friends until they have abandoned their homes to fight for Allah's cause [jihad]. But if they turn back, find them and kill them wherever they are.*

The whole world must submit to Islam; Kafirs are the enemy simply by not being Muslims. Violence and terror are made sacred by the Koran. Peace comes only with submission to Islam.

Political Islam, jihad, is universal and eternal.

> *[Muslim 001,0031] Mohammed: "I have been ordered to wage war against mankind until they accept that there is no god but Allah and that they believe I am His prophet and accept all revelations spoken through me. When they do these things I will protect their lives and property unless otherwise justified by Sharia, in which case their fate lies in Allah's hands."*

> *[Bukhari 4,52,142] Mohammed: "To battle Kafirs in jihad for even one day is greater than the entire earth and everything on it. A spot in Paradise smaller than your riding crop is greater than the entire earth and everything on it. A day or a night's travel in jihad is greater than the entire world and everything on it."*

09.1 THE OBLIGATORY CHARACTER OF JIHAD

Jihad is a communal obligation. When enough people perform it, it is no longer obligatory upon others.

Koran 4:95 *Believers who stay at home in safety, other than those who are disabled, are not equal to those who fight with their wealth and their lives for Allah's cause [jihad].*

> *[Bukhari 4,52,96] Mohammed: "Anyone who arms a jihadist is rewarded just as a fighter would be; anyone who gives proper care to a holy warrior's dependents is rewarded just as a fighter would be."*

WHO IS OBLIGED TO FIGHT IN JIHAD

09.4 All sane able bodied men who have reached puberty.

THE OBJECTIVES OF JIHAD

09.8 The caliph (supreme ruler who is both a king and similar to a pope) makes war on the Jews and Christians. First invite them to Islam, then invite them to pay the jizya (tax on Kafirs). If they reject conversion and the jizya, then attack them.

Koran 9:29 *Make war on those who have received the Scriptures [Jews and Christians] but do not believe in Allah or in the Last Day. They do not forbid what Allah and His Messenger have forbidden. The Christians and Jews do not follow the religion of truth until they submit and pay the poll tax [jizya] and they are humiliated.*

09.9 The caliph fights all other peoples [Kafirs] until they become Muslims.

THE SPOILS OF WAR

010.2 Anyone who kills or incapacitates a Kafir, can take whatever he can.

> *[Bukhari 4,53,351] Mohammed: "Allah has made it legal for me to take spoils of war."*

Koran 8:41 *Know that a fifth of all your spoils of war [the traditional cut for the leader was a fourth] belong to Allah, to His messenger, to the messenger's family, the orphans, and needy travelers.*

Since jihad can be done by Muslims against any Kafir, with the proper motivation, theft from a Kafir is jihad.

DYING IN JIHAD—MARTYRDOM

A Muslim martyr is one who kills for Allah and Islam. But his killing must be pure and devoted only to Allah. If his motivation is pure, then the jihadist will achieve Paradise or be able to take the wealth of the Kafir.

> *[**Bukhari 1,2,35**] Mohammed said, "The man who joins jihad, compelled by nothing except sincere belief in Allah and His Prophets, and survives, will be rewarded by Allah either in the afterlife or with the spoils of war. If he is killed in battle and dies a martyr, he will be admitted into Paradise. ..."*

Koran 61:10 *Believers! Should I show you a profitable exchange that will keep you from severe torment? Believe in Allah and His messenger and fight valiantly for Allah's cause [jihad] with both your wealth and your lives. It would be better for you, if you only knew it!*

THE EFFECTIVENESS OF JIHAD

In Mecca Mohammed was a religious preacher who converted about 10 people a year to Islam. In Medina Mohammed was a warrior and politician who converted about 10,000 people to Islam every year. Politics and jihad were a thousand times more effective than religion to convert the Arabs to Islam. If Mohammed had not taken to politics and jihad, there would have only been a few hundred Muslims when he died and Islam would have failed. The religion of Islam was a failure, but politics combined with religion was a total success.

The graph clearly shows the growth of Islam during its two phases.

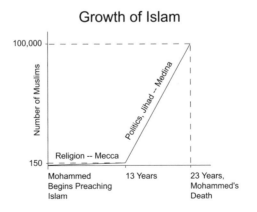

23

THE STATISTICS OF JIHAD

Jihad takes up a large portion of the Trilogy. Jihad verses are 24% of the later, political Koran and average 9% of the total of the entire Koran. Jihad takes up 21% of the Bukhari Hadith material and the Sira devotes 67% of its text to jihad[1]. Notice how the dualism of the Koran is demonstrated by the Mecca and Medina content about jihad. The Koran of Mecca does not have any jihad and it is the Meccan Koran we see referenced by Muslims and their apologists.

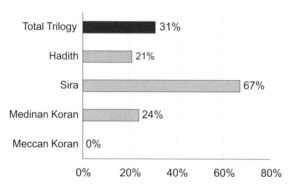

Amount of Trilogy Text Devoted to Jihad

THE TEARS OF JIHAD

Here are the deaths due to jihad over the last 1400 years[2]:

Christians .... 60 million
Hindus .... 80 million
Buddhists .... 10 million
Africans .... 120 million

Total .... 270 million

These deaths are called the Tears of Jihad.

---

1   http://cspipublishing.com/statistical/TrilogyStats/Percentage_of_Trilogy_Text_Devoted_to_Jihad.html
2   *The Submission of Women and Slaves*, CSPI Publishing, page 181.

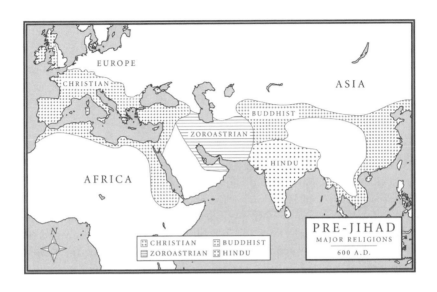

PRE-JIHAD
MAJOR RELIGIONS
600 A.D.

CHRISTIAN   BUDDHIST
ZOROASTRIAN   HINDU

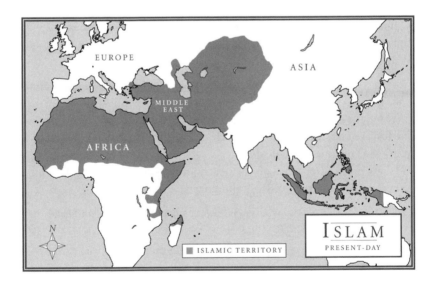

ISLAM
PRESENT-DAY

ISLAMIC TERRITORY

SUBMISSION AND DUALISM

CHAPTER 7

SUBMISSION

Since Sharia is based on the Koran and the Sunna of Mohammed, it is inevitable that Sharia would contain the same fundamental principles. The first principle of Islam is that the entire world must submit to Allah and follow the Sunna of Mohammed. This implies that Muslims must submit to the Sharia. The Kafir is subjugated in every mention in the Sharia. There is no equality between a Muslim and a Kafir; the Kafir is politically an inferior.

Sharia demands that our institutions submit to Islam. Our schools must submit in how they teach about Islam. Our media must present Islam in a good light. Every facet of our civilization must submit. What this means on a daily basis is that if Islam has a demand such as school prayer, we must do as they ask.

Jihad is a demand for total submission and if the Kafir does not willingly submit, then force may be used. The dhimmi must submit in a formal way to political Islam.

DUALISM

The Kafir and jihad are part of Sharia. Sharia holds two sets of laws—one for Muslims and one for Kafirs. Kafirs are not treated as equals, but as inferiors. This is legal dualism.

Islam holds two views about nearly every subject relating to Kafirs. Here is a tolerant example from the Koran:

> Koran 73:10 *Listen to what they [Kafirs] say with patience, and leave them with dignity.*

From tolerance we move to intolerance:

> Koran 8:12 *Then your Lord spoke to His angels and said, "I will be with you. Give strength to the believers. I will send terror into the Kafirs' hearts, cut off their heads and even the tips of their fingers!"*

The Koran is so filled with contradictions such as this that it provides a method to resolve the problem, called abrogation.

Abrogation means that the later verse is stronger than the earlier verse. However, both verses are still true, since the Koran is the exact, precise word of Allah. In the two verses above, the first verse is earlier than the second verse and is, therefore, weaker. It is always that way. The early, weaker "good" verse is abrogated by the later, stronger "bad" verse.

The "truth" of the earlier Meccan verses is demonstrated by the fact that it is the Meccan Koran that is quoted by Muslims and apologists. It may be abrogated, but it is still used as the sacred truth of the Koran.

Practically speaking, this means that the early verses are used when Islam is weak and the later verses are used when Islam is strong. This parallels Mohammed's life.

Mohammed's career had two distinctly different phases—early and late. In Mecca Mohammed was a religious preacher. Later, in Medina he became a politician and warrior and became very powerful. The early Meccan Koran gives the advice of Allah when Islam is weak and the later Medinan Koran says what to do when Islam is strong. The stronger Mohammed became, the harder he waged war against the Kafirs. The Koran gives the proper advice to every Muslim for every stage.

Effectively, there are two Mohammeds and two Korans that contradict each other. The early religious peaceful Koran of Mecca is contradicted by the later, political, jihad Koran of Medina. But it is still true and can be used. These early verses are the ones we hear by supporters of Islam.

Since Mohammed's actions are the perfect pattern of behavior, his actions establish Islam's dualistic ethics.

Dualism gives Islam an incredible flexibility and adaptability.

DUALISTIC ETHICS

Islam does not have a Golden Rule. The very existence of the word "kafir" in a sacred text means that there is no Golden Rule, because no one wants to be treated as Kafirs were treated by Mohammed. Kafirs were murdered, tortured, enslaved, raped, robbed, deceived, mocked and ridiculed.

> *[Bukhari 9,85,83] Mohammed: "A Muslim is a brother to other Muslims. He should never oppress them nor should he facilitate their oppression. Allah will satisfy the needs of those who satisfy the needs of their brothers."*

Islam does not have a common ethic for humanity, instead it has dualistic ethics. There are two sets of rules: a Muslim is a brother to another Muslim. A Muslim may treat a Kafir as a brother or as an enemy.

Also in Islam, something that is not true is not always a lie.

> *[Bukhari 3,49,857] Mohammed: "A man who brings peace to the people by making up good words or by saying nice things, though untrue, does not lie."*

An oath by a Muslim is flexible.

> *[Bukhari 8,78,618] Abu Bakr faithfully kept his oaths until Allah revealed to Mohammed the atonement for breaking them. Afterwards he said, "If I make a pledge and later discover a more worthy pledge, then I will take the better action and make amends for my earlier promise."*

Mohammed repeatedly told Muslims to deceive Kafirs, when it would advance Islam.

> *[Bukhari 5,59,369] Mohammed asked, "Who will kill Ka'b, the enemy of Allah and Mohammed?"*
>
> *Bin Maslama rose and responded, "O Mohammed! Would it please you if I killed him?"*
>
> *Mohammed answered, "Yes."*
>
> *Bin Maslama then said, "Give me permission to deceive him with lies so that my plot will succeed."*
>
> *Mohammed replied, "You may speak falsely to him."*
>
> *[Bukhari 4, 52, 268] Mohammed said, "Jihad is deceit."*

Islam has a word for deception that advances its goals: *taqiyya*. Taqiyya is sacred deception. But a Muslim must never lie to another Muslim. A lie should never be told unless there is no other way to accomplish the task. Al Tabarani, in *Al Awsat*, said, "Lies are sins except when they are told for the welfare of a Muslim or for saving him from a disaster." [1]

FRIENDS

Islamic dualistic ethics includes the doctrine of friends. There are 12 verses in the Koran which state that a Muslim is not the friend of a Kafir. Here are two examples:

> **Koran 4:144** *Believers! Do not take Kafirs as friends over fellow believers. Would you give Allah a clear reason to punish you?*

---

1. Bat Ye'or, *The Dhimmi* (Cranbury, N.J.: Associated University Presses, 2003), 392.

Koran 3:28 *Believers should not take Kafirs as friends in preference to other believers. Those who do this will have none of Allah's protection and will only have themselves as guards. Allah warns you to fear Him for all will return to Him.*

ENSLAVEMENT

Dualism dictates that a Kafir may be enslaved, but it is forbidden to enslave a Muslim. If a slave converts to Islam, then there is a benefit in freeing him, but there is no benefit in freeing a Kafir slave.

> *[Bukhari 3,46,693] Mohammed said, "If a man frees a Muslim slave, Allah will free him from the fires of Hell in the same way that he freed the slave." Bin Marjana said that, after he related that revelation to Ali, the man freed a slave for whom he had been offered one thousand dinars by Abdullah.*

AL WALAA WA AL BARAA—SACRED LOVE AND SACRED HATE

The Sharia teaches the dualistic ethical principle of "loving what Allah loves and hating what Allah hates" (see page 18). This includes having an aversion to Kafir political systems, such as Constitutional law and loving Sharia law. This principle is behind the Islamic demands for implementation of Sharia in America. No matter what the Kafir way is, it is not to be imitated, since Allah hates all manifestations of Kafirs.

THE DHIMMI

ISLAMIC SCHOLARS CLAIM: Islam is a brother religion to Christianity and Judaism; under Islamic rule Christians and Jews who become dhimmis are cared for and protected.

When Mohammed moved to Medina, it was half Jewish and he annihilated them. Then he turned his attentions to the wealthy Jews of Khaybar. He attacked them all without provocation and crushed them. They lost all of their wealth and were left in a third-class political status as dhimmis. The Jews were subject to Sharia, lost all political power, but they could still be Jews. As dhimmis they had to pay a yearly tax called the *jizya*, half of their income.

From the Sharia:

O11.0 KAFIR SUBJECTS OF THE ISLAMIC STATE

o11.1 A formal contract (dhimma) is made with Christians and Jews, but not Mormons[1]. They then become dhimmis.

o11.3 The dhimmis must follow the rules of Islam.

- Pay the jizya, the dhimmi poll tax.
- If the dhimmis do these things, then they are protected by the state. They are allowed to practice their religions, hold their own courts, and laws.

Here are the complete Sharia dhimmi rules taken from a treaty with Christians in 637 AD. The rules are similar for Jews and others.

The Treaty of Umar

We shall not build, in our cities or in their neighborhood new monasteries, churches, convents, or monks' cells, nor shall we repair, by day or by night, such of them as fall in ruins or are situated in the quarters of the Muslims.

We shall keep our gates wide open for passersby and travelers. We shall give board and lodging to all Muslims who pass our way for three days.

---

1 *Traveller* was written in the 14th century, Mormons are a later interpolation.

We shall not give shelter in our churches or in our dwellings to any spy nor hide him from the Muslims.

We shall not manifest our religion publicly nor convert anyone to it.

We shall not prevent any of our kin from entering Islam if they wish it.

We shall show respect toward the Muslims, and we shall rise from our seats when they wish to sit.

We shall not seek to resemble the Muslims by imitating any of their garments.

We shall not mount on saddles, nor shall we gird swords nor bear any kind of arms nor carry them on our persons.

We shall not engrave Arabic inscriptions on our seals.

We shall not sell fermented drinks (alcohol).

We shall clip the fronts of our heads (keep a short forelock as a sign of humiliation).

We shall always dress in the same way wherever we may be, and we shall bind the zunar round our waists. (Christians and Jews had to wear special clothing.)

We shall not display our crosses or our books in the roads or markets of the Muslims. We shall only use clappers in our churches very softly. We shall not raise our voices when following our dead. We shall not take slaves who have been allotted to Muslims.

We shall not build houses higher than the houses of the Muslims.

Whoever strikes a Muslim with deliberate intent shall forfeit the protection of this pact.

(from Al-Turtushi, *Siraj Al-Muluk*, p. 229-30)

In addition, the dhimmi could not testify in a Sharia court and, therefore, had no legal recourse in an argument with a Muslim. A dhimmi could not criticize Mohammed or speak with a Muslim about Christianity.

The Sharia and the dhimmi explain how the Christian nations of Turkey, Egypt, North Africa, Lebanon, Syria, Iraq and Ethiopia became Islamic. Jihad placed Muslims in political control and established Sharia law. Then all of the Christians became dhimmis. Centuries of the jizya tax and third-class status caused them to convert. It was Sharia law and the dhimmi status that destroyed Christianity in Islamic lands. Western civilization cannot survive under Sharia law.

SLAVERY

CHAPTER 9

SHARIA: The current version of the manual on Sharia, *The Reliance of the Traveller*, contains a vestige of Islam's extensive doctrine of slavery. Section k 32.0, Manumission, of the Sharia is left without translation. Instead there is an editorial apology about slavery as something that Islam set about to abolish as soon as possible. This is pure *taqiyya*, sacred deceit. Islam has been the most powerful enslaver of any and all ideologies. Islam was built on slavery.

MOHAMMED AND SLAVERY

The term *slave* is a positive one in Islam. Mohammed referred to himself and Muslims as the slaves of Allah. Mohammed's second convert was a slave.

Mohammed himself was involved in every single aspect of slavery. He had non-believing men killed so their women and children could be made slaves[1]. He gave slaves away for gifts[2]. He owned many slaves, some of them black[3]. He passed around slaves for the purpose of sex to his companions, men who were his chief lieutenants[4]. He stood by while others beat slaves[5]. He shared the pleasure of forced sex with women slaves after conquest[6]. He captured slaves and wholesaled them to raise money for jihad[7]. One of his favorite sexual partners was a slave, who bore him a son[8]. He got slaves as gifts from other rulers[9]. The very pulpit he preached from was made by

---

1. A. Guillaume, *The Life of Muhammad* (London: Oxford University Press, 1982), 466.
2. Ibid., p. 499.
3. Ibid., p. 516.
4. Ibid., p. 593.
5. Ibid., p. 295.
6. Ibid., p. 496.
7. Ibid., p. 466.
8. William Muir, *The Life of Mohammed* (AMS Press, 1975), 425.
9. Ibid., p. 425.

a slave[10]. He ate food prepared by slaves[11]. He was treated medically by a slave[12]. He had a slave tailor[13]. He declared that a slave who ran away from his master would not have his prayers answered[14]. And he approved of an owner's having sex with his slaves[15].

ISLAM AND SLAVERY

Islam enslaved Africans, Europeans (over a million of them), Hindus, Buddhists, and anyone else who was in the path of jihad. Islam has enslaved more people than any other culture. Muslims do not acknowledge and apologize for their history of enslavement of all races and faiths.

A little known fact is that the highest priced slave in Mecca was always a white woman. The Sunna is that Mohammed's favorite sex-slave was a white Christian woman.

Islam still practices slavery in Africa. It is found in Saudi Arabia, Mauritania, the Sudan and other Islamic areas that are near Kafirs.

Historically, it was the political actions of Christians that ended slavery[16].

---

10. Bukhari, Hadith, Volume 1, Book 8, Number 440.

11. Ibid., Volume 3, Book 34, Number 295.

12. Ibid., Volume 3, Book 36, Number 481.

13. Ibid., Volume 7, Book 65, Number 344.

14. *Muslim*, Hadith, Book 001, Number 0131.

15. Ibid., Book 008, Number 3383.

16. Bernard Lewis, *Race and Slavery in the Middle East*, Oxford University Press, 1990, page 79.

FREEDOM OF IDEAS

CHAPTER 10

CLAIM: Islam is a religion of tolerance.

THE SHARIA: Apostasy means to leave Islam; for a Muslim to leave Islam is a capital crime, punishable by death.

08.0 APOSTASY FROM ISLAM

08.1 When a person who has reached puberty and is sane, voluntarily apostatizes from Islam, he deserves to be killed.

In Islam the option of killing an apostate, one who leaves Islam, is spelled out in the Hadith and the early history of Islam after Mohammed's death.

When Mohammed died, entire tribes wanted to leave Islam. The first wars fought by Islam were against these apostates, and thousands were killed.

> *[Bukhari 2,23,483] After the death of Mohammed, Abu Bakr became the caliph, and he declared war against a group of Arabs who reverted back to paganism.*

> *[Bukhari 9,83,17] Mohammed: "A Muslim who has admitted that there is no god but Allah and that I am His prophet may not be killed except for three reasons: as punishment for murder, for adultery, or for apostasy."*

No punishment is too great for the apostate.

> *[Bukhari 8,82,797] Some people came to Medina and became Muslims. They became ill, so Mohammed sent them to the place where the camels were sheltered and told them to drink camel urine and milk as a remedy. They followed his advice, but when they recovered, they killed the shepherd guarding the camels and stole the herd.*
>
> *In the morning, Mohammed heard what the men had done and ordered their capture. Before noon, the men were captured and brought before Mohammed. He ordered that their hands and feet be cut off and their eyes gouged out with hot pokers. They were then*

thrown on jagged rocks, their pleas for water ignored and they died of thirst.

Abu said, "They were thieves and murderers who abandoned Islam and reverted to paganism, thus attacking Allah and Mohammed."

Kill the apostate.

[Bukhari 9,89,271] A certain Jew accepted Islam, but then reverted to his original faith. Muadh saw the man with Abu Musa and said, "What has this man done?"

Abu Musa answered, "He accepted Islam, but then reverted to Judaism."

Muadh then said, "It is the verdict of Allah and Mohammed that he be put to death and I'm not going to sit down unless you kill him."

The idea of freedom of religion and thought is impossible in Islam. Submission is the key idea and the ideal citizen is a slave of Allah. All thought must submit to the Koran and the Sunna—Sharia law.

ART

There is no limit to the extent and detail of Sharia law. All public expressions of ideas and art must submit to Sharia's prohibitions.

R40.0 MUSIC, SONG, AND DANCE—MUSICAL INSTRUMENTS

r40.1 Musical instruments are to be done away with.
- Flutes, stringed instruments and the like are condemned
- Those who listen to singers will have their ears filled with lead on Judgment day
- Songs create hypocrisy

r40.2 It is unlawful to use musical instruments or listen to the mandolin, lute, cymbals, and flute. It is permissible to play the tambourine at weddings, circumcisions, and other times, even if it has bells on its sides. Beating drum is unlawful

W50.0 THE PROHIBITION OF DEPICTING ANIMATE LIFE

w50.1 One should realize that the prohibition of picture making is extremely severe.

[Bukhari 7,72,843] Mohammed grew depressed one day after Gabriel's promised visit was delayed. When Gabriel came at last, Mohammed complained about the delay. Gabriel said to him, "Angels will not enter a house that contains a dog or a picture."

IMITATING THE CREATIVE ACT OF ALLAH

w50.2 Pictures imitate the creative act of Allah.

[Bukhari 4,54,447] One time I [Aisha] created a stuffed pillow for Mohammed and decorated it with pictures of animals. He came in with some other people one day, and I noticed a look of excitement on his face. I asked, "What is wrong?" He replied, "What is that pillow doing here?" I answered, "I made that for you so that you could lie on it." He said, "Are you not aware that angels will not enter a house with pictures in it and that the person that makes such pictures will be punished on Judgment Day until he gives life to that which he has made?"

P44.0 MAKING PICTURES

p44.1 Those who make pictures will burn in Hell.

[Bukhari 8,73,130] There was once a curtain with pictures of animals on it in my [Aisha's] house. When Mohammed saw it, his face became flushed with anger. He tore it to bits and said, "People that paint such pictures will receive Hell's most terrible punishment on Judgment Day."

LITERATURE

All literature must submit to the demands of Sharia. Those who offend Islam may be assassinated, since Mohammed had several artists assassinated. Salman Rushdie has lived under a death threat for writing a novel, *The Satanic Verses.* There were world wide riots and killings when the Danish Mohammed cartoons were published. Theo Van Gogh and Pim Fortun, two artists, were assassinated in Europe for "blasphemy" against Islam.

Mohammed repeatedly killed artists and intellectuals such as Kab, a poet, who wrote a poem criticizing Islam. Notice the use of deceit.

[Bukhari 5,59,369] Allah's Apostle said, "Who is willing to kill Kab who has hurt Allah and His Apostle?"
Thereupon Maslama got up saying, "O Allah's Apostle! Would you like that I kill him?"

The Prophet said, "Yes."

Maslama said, "Then allow me to say a false thing to deceive Kab."

The Prophet said, "You may say it."

Then Maslama went to Kab and said, "Mohammed demands money from us and I need to borrow money."

On that, Kab said, "By Allah, you will get tired of him!"

Maslama said, "Now as we have followed him, we do not want to leave him. Now we want you to lend us a camel load of food."

Kab said, "Yes, I will lend you the food, but you should mortgage something to me."

They mortgaged their arms to him and promised to return that night. So Maslama returned with two men and said to them, "When Kab comes, I will touch his hair and smell it and, when you see that I have got hold of his head, kill him."

Kab came down to them wrapped in his clothes and smelling of perfume.

Maslama said, "I have never smelt a better scent than this. Will you allow me to smell your head?"

Kab said, "Yes."

When Maslama got a strong hold of him, he said to his companion, "Get at him!"

So they killed him and went to the Prophet and informed him. Abu Rafi was killed after Kab Bin Al-Ashraf.

Ishaq819 Mohammed had told his commanders only to kill those who resisted; otherwise they were not to bother anyone except for those who had spoken against Mohammed. He then issued death warrants for all of those in Mecca who had resisted Islam. The list of those to be killed was:

- One of Mohammed's secretaries. He had said that Mohammed sometimes let him insert better speech when he was recording Mohammed's Koranic revelations, and this caused the secretary to lose faith.
- Two girls who had sung satires against Mohammed.
- A Muslim tax collector who had become an apostate (left Islam).
- A man who had insulted Mohammed.
- All artists and political figures who had opposed him.

SHARIA FINANCE

CHAPTER 11

ISLAMIC SCHOLARS CLAIM: Sharia finance is sacred finance and all religious and moral people should invest in Sharia financial instruments. The money will not be invested in liquor, tobacco, gambling, pork, art or any other impure businesses.

Today there is an increasing demand for Muslims to have their own financial system and Sharia compliant financial products. Sharia finance uses a work-around to avoid paying interest, which is illegal in Islam. It turns out that Sharia finance actually charges more for the use of money, but it is not called interest, it is termed a leasing cost.

THE SHARIA: Sharia finance must put part of its profits into the zakat, Islamic charity. The zakat must be used for the following:

> Koran 9:60 *Charity [the zakat] is only to be given to the poor and needy, to those who collect them, to those whose hearts are won to Islam, for ransoms, for debtors, for fighting in Allah's cause [jihad], and for the traveler. This is a law from Allah, and Allah is knowing and wise.*

Sharia devotes pages to the zakat. It is to be paid to:

- Poor and needy Muslims, but not to kafirs
- Those who collect the zakat
- New converts to Islam (to strengthen them in Islam)
- To ransom prisoners and slaves
- Fighting in Allah's cause, jihad
- Travelers

THOSE FIGHTING FOR ALLAH

h8.17 The category *fighting for Allah's cause*, means people engaged in Islamic war, but who are not part of a regular army and receive a salary. These jihadists must be paid for weapons, clothing, meals, and travel and all other expenses. Their families should be paid as well.

h8.24 It is not permissible to give zakat to a Kafir.

When we participate in Sharia finance, we support:

- Charity for Muslims *only* with no charity going to Kafirs.
- Strengthening Muslim converts.
- Muslim bureaucrats.
- Al Qaeda and other jihadists. This includes money to the families of "suicide bombers" or any other jihadists who are killed

Giving zakat money for jihad is not a theory. We saw the practical effects of the zakat with the Holy Land Foundation and other Islamic charities. In 2007, in Dallas, Texas, the FBI successfully prosecuted the Holy Land Foundation for financing jihad (terrorism).

When we participate in Sharia finance, or any other aspect of Sharia, we are morally part of the rest:

- Abuse and subjugation of women
- Killing of apostates
- Assassination of artists and writers
- The ethical crime of unrepentant slavery
- Third class citizenship in politics for Kafirs
- The murder of 270 million people in the Tears of Jihad

EASE AND NECESSITY

Sharia has two principles which can be called "ease" and "necessity" (see page 41). Fundamentally, ease and necessity means that if a Muslim lives amongst Kafirs, the Muslim can do business the Kafir way.

W43.0 DEALING WITH INTEREST IN ENEMY LANDS

w43.1 Muslims can pay interest if they live in *dar al harb*, the land of war (amongst Kafirs), meaning the Sharia is not the law of the land.

Hence, Muslims can pay and receive interest in America, according to Sharia. So why do Muslims want Sharia financing? Simple. The principle of submission comes into play. Kafirs must submit to Sharia in all matters, including banking. Also, sacred love and sacred hate (pages 18, 29), means that our Kafir financial system must be destroyed.

Notice that according to Sharia, America is "enemy land".

DEMANDS

CHAPTER 12

MUSLIM LEADERS CLAIM: in order for us to practice our religion, you must give us our prayer in school; prayer in the workplace, rooms set aside in schools and workplaces for prayer, special food (*halal*); days off for Muslim holidays; head scarves at work and school and allow full body burkas in sports. Kafirs must never criticize any aspect of Islam, such as polygamy, jihad or wife-beating. Kafirs must furnish welfare support for our many wives, give special treatment to Muslim women in hospitals, and on and on.

THE SHARIA

The Sharia lays out the complete process and strategy of immigration into a Kafir nation and what to do to Islamicize the society. If you want to see the future of Islam in America, read the Sira (biography of Mohammed) of 1400 years ago.

When Muslims first arrive, they accept their new home. Their first step is to announce that Islam is a brother religion to Christianity and Judaism. Dialogues and "bridge building" sessions are held for the media and Kafir community. They also claim that Western Civilization is actually based on Islam's Golden Age.

After these claims are in place and accepted come the demands for changes in the Kafir nation. Those who resist these changes are called bigots, Islamophobes and racists, even though it is never made clear why resisting Political Islam has anything to do with race.

THE KAFIR LEADERS

Kafir leaders know nothing about Islam and Sharia law. They all have met nice Muslims, so they think that Islam must be good and the trouble makers must be extremists.

Kafir leaders know nothing about dualistic ethics or political submission. The prime motivation of Kafir leaders is to be nice and play the role of tolerant host to these new guests. A second motivation is not to say or do anything that will cause them to be labeled a bigot.

The master plan of Kafir leadership is that if we are nice, Muslims will see how good we are and will reform Islam. But, if your goal is to implement Sharia law and the process of applying Sharia law has worked without fail for 1400 years, why reform what is not broken?

Sharia cannot be reformed. It is Allah's law, and it is perfect, universal, complete and perfect.

SACRED LOVE AND SACRED HATE

The emotional motivation behind Islam's demands is "sacred hate", *al Walaa wa al Baraa* (pages 18, 29). Allah hates the Kafirs, their culture and politics. Therefore, anyone who loves Allah must hate what Allah hates and also must then have an aversion to our laws and Constitution. Hence, Islam must constantly make demands that Kafirs submit to Sharia.

FIRST AMENDMENT

Islam is a religion and Muslims have Freedom of Religion under our First Amendment. To deny any of Islam's religious demands is unconstitutional, so we must do whatever they ask, if it is religious.

But every "religious" demand by Islam has a political component. Here we have Mohammed's special gifts from Allah:

> *[Bukhari 1,7,331] Mohammed: I have been given five things which were not given to any one else before me:*
> *1. Allah made me victorious by awe, by His frightening my enemies for a distance of one month's journey.*
> *2. The earth has been made for me and for my followers, a place for praying and a place to perform rituals; therefore, anyone of my followers can pray wherever the time of a prayer is due.*
> *3. The spoils of war has been made lawful for me yet it was not lawful for anyone else before me.*
> *4. I have been given the right of intercession on the Day of Resurrection.*
> *5. Every Prophet used to be sent to his nation only but I have been sent to all mankind.*

The role of Islamic prayer is a political demand along with jihad and Sharia. Islam demands that the state serve its every need. This demand is the demand for political submission by Kafir governments.

Kafirs must learn the difference between religion and politics. The jihad attack on the World Trade Center was a political act with a religious motivation.

The innocent victims in the Towers who jumped to their death rather than be burned alive were not taking part in a religious ceremony.

When Muslims commandeer the public streets to pray, the prayer may be religious, but taking over the street is purely political.

The demand for Sharia law in all forms, including Muslim school prayer for instance, calls for us to take political action, issue directives to school boards, spend tax dollars in meetings, etc. The act of prayer may be religious, but it requires a political action and support of the state to happen.

Islamic prayer has a religious motivation and a political result. It is a demand for submission of the body politic by an ideology that is fundamentally in opposition to American law, culture and tradition.

We should react to all of Islam's political demands with a political response.

MAKING IT EASY AND NECESSITY

Kafirs do not have to accommodate Islam's demands.

The Sharia has two principles that provide guidance in the situation when Muslims cannot practice their pure Islam under Sharia. The technical name is *tayseer*, meaning "lightening one's burden" or "making it easy".

Koran 4:28 *Allah wishes to lighten your burden, for man was created weak.*

When the circumstances are difficult and Sharia law is not in force, a Muslim's burden is lightened. They are obligated to pray and not handle pork, for instance, but if the circumstances are difficult, then the requirements are lightened. This leads to the concept of *darura*, necessity.

If it is necessary, what is forbidden is permitted. If a Muslim is hungry and there is no *halal* (Sharia compliant) food, then he can eat any food. If a Muslim is where they cannot pray, then the prayer can be done later. If Sharia law has not been implemented, then a Muslim may handle pork, for example, with no consequences.

Here is an example of the principle of *darura*:

f15.17 It is a necessary condition for the permissibility of joining prayers (making up missed prayers) that the person be:
[...]
(5) Someone who fears harm in earning his living.

In short, if a Muslim cannot pray at work or school, it can be made up later. Islamic demands are about "wants" not necessities. If their demands are not met, there is no harm to their religion.

Another example of *darura* is found in buying insurance. Insurance is forbidden in Sharia, but if car insurance is required by Kafir law, then necessity allows a Muslim to buy the forbidden insurance.

By banning Sharia law, no Muslim's needs are violated. We are restricting Political Islam, not restricting religious Islam.

When we say no to Sharia prayer at school, we are not limiting any religious freedoms, we are protecting Kafir citizens against Islam's political demands. If a Muslim cannot pray at the appointed times, then Sharia law allows the prayer to be made up later. There is no harm in delaying prayer. Mohammed delayed prayer, hence all Muslims can delay prayer.

If Islamic prayer is allowed in school, how far does the prayer accommodation go? There are many elements—preparation, a special room, ritual bathing and special days that demand different prayers and longer times. In the final form of Islamic prayer, the room must be used only for Islamic prayer and special plumbing will have to be installed for the proper foot bathing for Islamic prayer.

Meanwhile, what does the teacher do when the students are gone to pray? If the teacher gives some information that is needed on the next test, does that discriminate against Islam? Why should the state have to pay for the room and foot baths for Islam?

The prayer is not a private affair. Islamic organizations will have to come and "explain" about Islam to the students.

Once Islamic prayer is in place, what is to stop the demand that the kitchen at the school become *halal* (Sharia complaint)? Why should the Kafir students eat while Ramadan fasting is going on? Since fasting weakens body and mind, should Muslims have to take tests during Ramadan? Should Muslim female athletes were Sharia compliant clothing (burka, hijab, ...) instead of school team clothing? Do not think this is an imaginary scenario. Submission to this process is underway in Britain today.

Then comes the demand for Sharia family law. After that comes the demand that Muslims be recognized as a "minority" and receive special treatment in appointments, jobs, and civil-rights. Then come Sharia courts. Once the thin end of the Sharia wedge is in place, there will be no end until there is full Sharia compliance for the nation and no Constitution.

ARTICLE SIX

Article 6 of the US Constitution states that the Constitution is the highest law of the land and cannot be subjugated to any other legal code. The fundamental claim of Sharia is that it is the highest law in the world and that all other legal codes must submit to Islamic law. There is a massive contradiction that is being ignored as Sharia law is being implemented under the guise of Freedom of Religion.

Islam's religion always has a political component that must be accommodated. As a contrasting example, there are as many Buddhists who have come to America just as Muslims have. Can you name a single political demand that Buddhists have made in the schools or any other area? Do you know of a case where Buddhists have made demands for coming into schools, businesses, law enforcement or hospitals and making demands that we learn about Buddhism and accommodate Buddhist practices? No, because Buddhism is a religion, not a political/religious ideology.

The religion of Islam demands that we make political accommodations, since Islam is a political ideology as well as a religion.

The Sharia attack on Article 6 is not direct, but it is a flanking attack. Take the example of freedom of speech and the press. When the Danish Mohammed cartoons were published, there were no major papers in the US that published them, since Muslims said that the cartoons were blasphemy and offended Islam. The result was that we followed Sharia law and did not print the cartoons. What politician protested at Sharia law being implemented and our Constitution being weakened by submission to it?

Freedom of speech is being denied when anyone who criticizes Islam is called a bigot and an Islamophobe. Currently, the First Amendment is being used to destroy Article 6. Islamic political doctrine is being legitimized under the cover of religion.

As a Constitutional matter, no aspect of Sharia should be allowed.

APPENDIX

STATISTICAL STUDY OF ISLAMIC DOCTRINE

There is a large body of Islamic doctrine about the inequality between men and women. What is confusing to a non-Muslim is that the doctrine can be contradictory. Islamic dualism means that there are two choices, both equally true. A statistical study of the doctrine has been made, so that the entire picture can be seen.

Each verse or hadith can be judged on the position of the female in society. There are a number of verses that praise the mother above all men. There are many verses that say that women and men will be judged equally as to their actions on Judgment Day. In many cases there is no power relationship at all; it is a neutral reference.

The process for generating the charts below selects all of the text that contains a reference to the female. Then the female data is sorted into four categories: High status, equal status, low status and neutral. A neutral reference does not have any hierarchical information. A example of a neutral reference could be a woman's name in a list. Here is data from the Koran :

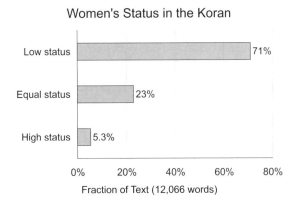

Women's Status in the Koran

45

Here is the same data analysis about the Hadith:

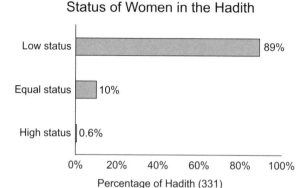

One of the foundations of Sharia law is the Koran. Since the Koran is the most famous book that has not been read or understood by Kafirs, this seems like a huge roadblock in learning about Sharia.

The Koran is actually easy to understand if you know one historical fact. We have a history of Mohammed's day and we find that illiterate Arabs not only understood the Koran, but they discussed its meaning.

They could do this because they were using a different Koran from the one you buy at the bookstore today. The Koran was produced years after Mohammed's death and it was arranged in order of chapter length for unknown reasons. Long chapters were placed at the beginning and the shortest chapters at the end. Imagine if you took a novel, cut off the spine and arranged the chapters in order of length. The novel would be destroyed since the plot would have been eliminated. The bookstore Koran has been randomized and makes no sense because it has no story or plot.

If you were a companion of Mohammed every verse made sense since it was in response to the situation Mohammed was in at the time. Each and every verse had a context and could be easily understood.

This historical Koran can be reconstructed. We have a highly detailed biography of Mohammed called the Sira. If we take the Sira and insert the appropriate Koran verses into his life, we will recreate the original Koran. Anyone can read and understand the historical Koran.

When this is done, it is clear that there are two very different Korans. The early Koran of Mecca is religious. The later Koran written in Medina

46

is very political. It is important to note that they frequently say things that contradict each other. This is the very foundation to Islamic dualism.

The historical Koran has a story. It begins with poetry about god. Then it declares war on every person who does not agree with Mohammed. It documents the annihilation of the native Kafir Arab culture of tolerance. In the end, all Arabians submitted in every detail to Sharia law. The political domination of Kafir Arabia to Islam was complete.

FOR MORE INFORMATION

www.politicalislam.com

READING LIST

THE SIRA

Mohammed and the Unbelievers, CSPI Publishing

THE HADITH

The Political Traditions of Mohammed, CSPI Publishing

THE KORAN

A Simple Koran or *An Abridged Koran*, CSPI Publishing

THE BEST ONE SOURCE BOOK FOR CHRISTIANS OR JEWS

The Third Choice, Mark Durie

WOMEN AND SHARIA

Cruel and Usual Punishment, Nonie Darwish

GENERAL INFORMATION

Stealth Jihad, Robert Spencer
Why I Am Not a Muslim, Ibn Warraq
They Must Be Stopped, Brigitte Gabriel